MINDFULNESS FOR MOTHERS

MINDFULNESS FOR MOTHERS

MARLOWE SINCLAIR

CONTENTS

CHAPTER 1

Introduction

"**The Mindful Mother: A Practical and Spiritual Guide to Enjoying Pregnancy, Birth, Your Baby, and Your Life in a New Way**" is a transformative work that invites parents to embrace the journey of motherhood with mindfulness and presence. Originally published in Danish and later translated into English, this guide transcends cultural boundaries, offering universal truths about the joys and challenges of parenting.

Mieko Muskett, a seasoned prenatal instructor and dedicated mother of one, opens the door to a deeper, more meaningful approach to parenting. She emphasizes that the most potent and rewarding way to experience a child's early years is by being fully present and engaged, rather than merely functioning on autopilot. According to Muskett, living mindfully as a mother can bring about profound benefits such as happiness, contentment, trust, love, camaraderie, and a profound appreciation for the present moment.

Muskett believes that a mindful mother is capable of achieving a state of calm, happiness, and contentment, along with the deep sense of love and satisfaction that every mother seeks. She argues that mindfulness allows mothers to navigate the complexities of life with grace and poise, providing a solid foundation for their children's growth and development.

In today's fast-paced world, mothers face unprecedented pressures. They are expected to excel in multiple roles – at work, at home, in marriages, friendships, and within their communities. This relentless drive often leads to a feeling of inadequacy in parenting. The harsh reality is that many mothers find themselves overextended, trying to juggle too many responsibilities and fearing that they are falling short in their parenting roles.

"The Mindful Mother" offers a refreshing perspective, reassuring mothers that while perfection is unattainable, peace is within reach. By adopting the principles of mindfulness, mothers can find balance and fulfillment, embracing the imperfections of motherhood with compassion and grace. This guide serves as a beacon of hope, showing that it is possible to enjoy pregnancy, birth, and the early years of motherhood in a profoundly new and enriching way.

CHAPTER 2

Understanding Mindfulness

Mindfulness practices have deep roots in ancient spiritual traditions, yet they transcend specific religious doctrines, making them accessible to everyone. Originating from Buddhist meditation teachings, mindfulness was born from a tradition focused on understanding reality and fostering spiritual well-being. These practices encourage individuals to cognitively accept that nothing in life is perfect. The goal is to recognize that our fears, anxieties, and struggles are integral parts of our experience. Through mindfulness, practitioners learn to integrate these challenges, thereby reducing their impact and changing physiological responses that perpetuate negative beliefs.

Mindfulness stems from the teachings of the Buddha and is deeply embedded in Buddhism. When we practice mindfulness, we become truly present in life's moments, disconnecting from automatic thoughts and immersing ourselves in the natural flow of our day. This practice is a valuable tool in the pursuit of happiness, freedom from anxiety and depression, successful conflict resolution, and improving overall well-being beyond the daily responsibilities of parenting. Mindfulness empowers us to use our thoughts constructively rather than being controlled by them.

In today's world, mindfulness is recognized as a non-religious discipline. It has seamlessly integrated into common psychotherapeutic practices and various Eastern religions. Skillful application of mindfulness can revolutionize our perceptions of stress and overburdened-ness, whether at home, in the office, or in any business dealings. By practicing mindfulness, we learn to navigate life's pressures with greater ease, turning our thoughts into allies instead of adversaries.

CHAPTER 3

Benefits of Mindfulness for Mothers

Mindful awareness empowers us to "see, and then be" – to observe the present moment and then use the wisdom gained to guide our actions. This concept, often referred to as the 'triple-A' or '3-C' plan, stands for **Right Attentiveness + Apperception = Appropriateness** (of action). In essence, it encapsulates the decision-making process: the ability to discern, to choose sides, and to apply our values. For mothers, this skill is crucial; it enables quick and accurate decisions, balancing empathy with necessary action in parenting. This approach supports effective negotiation between understanding our child's needs and making appropriate decisions that benefit both child and parent.

Respecting each moment as it unfolds teaches us to appreciate all that it brings – the joyful, the challenging, and even the exhausting. Mindful presence heightens our sensitivity to our children's emotions, fostering a healthy and nurturing parenting environment. In today's fast-paced world, this awareness is a precious gift we can offer our children. It transcends the desire for perfection and instead focuses on being truly present, offering our children the gift of our full attention and presence.

Even in a rapidly evolving society marked by technological advancements and increasing demands, mindfulness serves as a timeless practice. It helps us remain grounded, centered, and connected to our children, ensuring that we are not merely reacting to the chaos around us but responding thoughtfully and lovingly. This mindful presence not only benefits our children but also enhances our own well-being, creating a harmonious family dynamic.

Mindfulness also equips mothers with the resilience to handle the unpredictability of parenting. By embracing the present moment, we learn to navigate the uncertainties and challenges with grace and patience. This practice nurtures a deep sense of compassion for ourselves and our children, allowing us to be kinder, more understanding, and better equipped to face the daily demands of motherhood.

CHAPTER 4

Incorporating Mindfulness into Daily Life

While mindfulness is widely acknowledged for its effectiveness in stress reduction, the whirlwind of the postpartum period and early parenthood often makes it challenging to add another task to an already bustling schedule. Life with a newborn is incredibly flexible, adapting to the rhythms of the baby's wakeful and sleepy times. Free time becomes a precious commodity for mothers, who often find themselves juggling multiple demands, from diaper changes to preparing wholesome meals.

For every mother who passionately embraces mindfulness, there are countless demands that seem to compete for her attention. Thus, incorporating mindfulness into daily life requires intention, flexibility, and creative problem-solving. Mothers must learn to weave mindfulness into the natural pauses in their days, such as during naps or early bedtimes, rather than setting aside additional time specifically for practice.

When a mother begins to explore mindfulness, she discovers its profound potential. She starts to appreciate everything around her – as Thich Nhat Hanh famously states, "everything becomes the mint." She marvels at her body's ability to nurture and sustain new life, cherishing her belly that has stretched and accommodated her growing child. She savors the blissful moment when, after hours of labor, she cradles her newborn for the first time. She delights in the milky scent of the early postpartum days and the enveloping warmth of her newly expanded family.

Mindfulness allows a mother to find joy in the everyday moments that might otherwise go unnoticed. She learns to appreciate the piles of damp washcloths, recognizing them as a sign of the care and love she provides. This sense of appreciation soon blossoms into awe as she witnesses the miraculous changes and exquisite details of her baby. Each new discovery becomes a moment of mindfulness, grounding her in the present and deepening her connection to her child.

Through mindfulness, mothers can transform mundane tasks into moments of reflection and presence. Whether it's during a quiet feeding session, a peaceful walk with the stroller, or a bedtime story, mindfulness offers a way to be fully engaged with the experience. It fosters a deeper connection with their children and a greater sense of fulfillment in their role as a parent.

By integrating mindfulness into daily life, mothers can navigate the challenges of parenthood with greater ease and resilience. They become more attuned to their own needs and emotions, fostering a sense of inner peace that radiates throughout their family. Mindfulness becomes a valuable tool not only for managing stress but for enriching the entire parenting experience.

CHAPTER 5

Mindful Parenting Techniques

Stop Multitasking

Parenting can be overwhelming, especially when trying to juggle multiple tasks at once. Multitasking adds complexity and often results in us doing just the bare minimum to get through our tasks without truly enjoying any of them. We end up exhausted and wondering why our evenings are spent in a blur after a long day at work or managing household responsibilities.

Instead of spreading yourself thin, focus on one task at a time and give it your full attention. Whether you are disciplining a child, cleaning the house, or engaged in any other activity, approach it mindfully. Concentrate on the present task and aim to make it the best it can be. This focused approach not only enhances the quality of what you do but also brings a sense of fulfillment and calmness.

Mindful Mealtimes

Life changes dramatically when children begin eating solid foods or start experimenting with new foods around six months or later. Mealtime can become a challenging task, with children finding numerous ways to avoid eating. Whether you're chasing after a child to get them to eat or sitting down with them, it's essential to remind yourself that these moments are opportunities to create happy memories.

Engage with your child during mealtime. Enjoy their frustrations, curiosity, and the interest they show in their food. A mindful mealtime is more about the parent being present and engaged than about the child. Take this time to connect, talk, and make the experience enjoyable for both of you. This not only fosters a positive relationship with food but also strengthens your bond with your child.

Set Intentions for the Day

As you wake up each day, set a clear intention for the kind of parent you want to be. Even if you feel overwhelmed by chores, cooking, feeding, or cleaning, bringing a little mindfulness into your thoughts as you start your day can make a significant difference.

An intention might be, "I want to be present in the moment today," or "I want to set aside my mobile phone and other distractions to focus on my child when they need me." Setting an intention means recognizing all the tasks you need to accomplish but prioritizing what truly matters at that moment. This simple practice can help you approach your day with a clear focus, making it easier to handle the ups and downs of parenting with grace and patience.

CHAPTER 6

Nurturing Self-Compassion

Through mindfulness, we can illuminate our harsh self-expectations, finding both peace and the capacity for self-love. Self-compassion is a powerful and necessary component of well-being, emotional stability, and our emotional bond with our children. We must remember that before we can truly see those around us, we must first see ourselves. We need to be more flexible when faced with our own shortcomings and struggles. Only by accepting our own journey and current circumstances can we offer others the same capacity for self-acceptance, which is crucial in our roles as guides and mothers to our children.

If we do not work to accept ourselves with kindness and warmth, and instead respond to our struggles with self-criticism, we hinder the growth and development of our children. We deprive them of the natural security that comes when one of life's caregivers can love and accept themselves, and therefore, their children, as they are. Healing our hearts by learning to treat ourselves with a loving eye is a truly noble pursuit.

As mothers navigating what is often a high-pressure, fast-paced world, many of us struggle with self-criticism and self-doubt. The pace of life is exhausting, and mothers are often the last people in the family to receive attention. We put tremendous pressure on ourselves, striving to be perfect caregivers, to have our homes and families run smoothly, to earn enough money, to take care of our bodies, to maintain social relationships, and to be attractive. We also deal with societal expectations of what it means to be a good mother, and we internalize these ideals, carrying within our minds a set of rules and expectations that we believe we must meet to be loved, to be good mothers, or to do things "correctly."

Mindfulness helps us break free from these self-imposed rules and expectations. It encourages us to treat ourselves with the same compassion and understanding that we would offer to a friend. By practicing self-compassion, we learn to navigate the challenges of motherhood with greater ease and resilience. We allow ourselves to make mistakes, to learn from them, and to grow.

Incorporating self-compassion into our daily lives involves recognizing our own needs and giving ourselves permission to meet them. It means being gentle with ourselves when things don't go as planned and celebrating our successes, no matter how small. This practice not only enhances our own well-being but also sets a powerful example for our children. They learn to treat themselves with kindness and to approach life's challenges with a compassionate heart.

CHAPTER 7

Cultivating Gratitude

I am a flawed, unreasonable human creature. But having children has indeed opened my eyes to something I might have missed had I chosen not to join the motherhood ranks: gratitude. No, I am not grateful for sleepless nights and used Band-Aids stuck to the dining room table. I'm not homeless, hungry, or alone. I was determined not to be one of those beings who took life for granted, especially not from a being with a soft spot for offering reverence to the most astounding moments. It took some time and a lot of influential beings to tip me toward an existence where I can bask in the present moment, but I think I'm finally getting there. And if I can get there, then certainly—with enough intention and awareness—I can bring my children along to bask with me. Beyond gratitude, mindfulness also brings along its best friend: empathy. Through this journey of seeking truth, we are bound to find ourselves snuggled in the abundant pillow of kindness. And that journey, that divine quest toward understanding our deepest selves, begins with mindfulness.

I've always been a bit of a grumbler, I'll admit. When my first-born was a baby during a sweltering hot summer and I was on the verge of an emotional and physical breakdown from monthly mastitis and sleep deprivation, my poor husband innocently complimented me. "You're handling all of this so well," he said. Standing there in just my underwear, trailing baby-spit and mustard-colored diaper leaks, leaky boobs wreathed with warmth-induced rolls of maternal fat, I snapped at him with ungrateful frustration. "Well" seemed like a gross exaggeration, and I told him as much. "Just because I'm not throwing our baby in the trash and setting myself on fire doesn't mean I'm handling it well," I snapped. And we laughed. We laughed because it was actually funny; I have a way of taking a compliment, gargling shame through the rusty span of my ungrateful mouth, and spitting it back brackish onto the clean white dish of my conscience.

CHAPTER 8

Managing Stress and Anxiety

Ironically, to be fully present for our loved ones, we must first reconnect with ourselves and with nature. This reconnection restores the essence of what we share with those we care about. By grounding ourselves in the here and now, we find a sense of realization and presence that is truly transformative.

Embracing Nature and the Present Moment

Connecting with nature allows us to unite with our surroundings and distance ourselves from the flickering images of screens and the illusion of a world beyond our immediate touch. When our environment inspires us, we can genuinely connect and love. This disconnection from states of mind such as forgetfulness, dispersion, and anxiety helps us strengthen our spirit of compassion and reconciliation.

Offering Calm and Peace to Our Children

The realization of life, along with a sense of confirmation, calm, and peace in the present moment, is one of the greatest gifts we can offer our children. Like the work of a village elder, our role involves navigating today's events and situations to uncover the timeless, sacred moments of life.

Wisdom from Thích Nhất Hạnh

In deceptively minimalist language, Thích Nhất Hạnh outlines the essentials of mindful parenting. He teaches that by carefully attending to our partner's needs, we plant durable seeds of happiness and faithfulness in the heart of our companion. Adjusting our schedules to spend quality time and be present with our children is crucial, as parenthood is an art that demands our time and presence.

Practical Steps to Manage Stress and Anxiety

1. **Grounding Techniques**: Practice grounding techniques such as deep breathing, meditation, or a mindful walk in nature. These practices help center your mind and reduce stress.

2. **Mindful Breaks**: Take regular breaks throughout the day to check in with yourself. Use these moments to breathe deeply, stretch, and refocus your mind.

3. **Limit Screen Time**: Reduce exposure to screens and digital media. Allocate specific times for technology use and prioritize activities that promote relaxation and connection with nature.

4. **Prioritize Self-Care**: Make time for self-care activities that rejuvenate you, whether it's reading a book, taking a bath, or engaging in a hobby. Self-care is essential for maintaining your well-being.

5. **Communicate Needs**: Clearly communicate your needs and boundaries with your partner, family, and friends. Ensuring that you have support and understanding can significantly reduce stress.

6. **Practice Gratitude**: Cultivate a habit of gratitude by acknowledging the positive aspects of your day. This practice shifts your focus away from stressors and fosters a sense of appreciation.

7. **Engage in Physical Activity**: Regular physical activity, whether it's yoga, jogging, or a simple walk, can help alleviate stress and boost your mood.

By integrating these practices into your daily routine, you can manage stress and anxiety more effectively, creating a serene and supportive environment for both yourself and your family.

CHAPTER 9

Enhancing Emotional Well-being

The Power of Positive Affirmations

Studies have shown that self-criticism can lead to anxiety and depression. Through my research and personal practice, I've discovered that counteracting self-criticism with positive affirmations can significantly boost emotional well-being. Positive affirmations validate our courage and self-love, reminding us that we are deserving of our goals and that we are indeed valuable and meaningful individuals. This reminder of our value and meaningfulness creates space for natural growth towards self-improvement, ultimately enhancing our emotional well-being.

Embracing Creativity

Creativity is another powerful tool for boosting emotional well-being. Sharing your precious talents with your child not only nurtures their creativity but also enhances your own emotional well-being as a parent. Encourage their creativity and talents, as this mutual exchange fosters a sense of joy and fulfillment. Even if you are not a mother, understanding and engaging in the nurturing process, regardless of its form, invokes an innate desire to elevate the human spirit. Children, with their vulnerability and need, remind us of the sacramental aspects of life and help us appreciate life's beauty.

Practical Exercises for Enhancing Emotional Well-being

If you're looking to enhance your emotional well-being and positive feelings, here are a few key exercises to help increase your joy, boost your positivity, cultivate your talents, and give back to others:

1. **Practice Joy**: Joy is an essential aspect of emotional well-being. Finding ways to be more joyful will not only benefit your life but also the lives of your loved ones. Make a list of everyday things that bring you joy and incorporate them into your daily routine.

2. **Visualize Your Best Possible Future Self**: Studies have found that focusing on your best possible future self can boost your positivity, cultivate your talents, and help you overcome pessimism. Spend a few minutes each day visualizing the person you aspire to be and the goals you want to achieve.

3. **Positive Affirmations**: Start your day with positive affirmations that reinforce your self-worth and goals. Repeat phrases like "I am deserving of my goals" and "I am valuable and meaningful" to counteract self-criticism and promote self-love.

4. **Engage in Creative Activities**: Whether it's painting, writing, or playing an instrument, engage in creative activities that bring you joy and fulfillment. Share these activities with your child to strengthen your bond and boost your mutual well-being.

5. **Gratitude Practice**: Cultivate a habit of gratitude by acknowledging the positive aspects of your day. This practice shifts your focus away from stressors and fosters a sense of appreciation and positivity.

6. **Mindful Moments**: Take mindful moments throughout the day to check in with yourself. Use these moments to breathe deeply, reflect on your feelings, and reconnect with your inner self.

By integrating these exercises into your daily routine, you can enhance your emotional well-being, create a joyful and positive environment, and foster a deep sense of fulfillment.

CHAPTER 10

Improving Communication with Children

Valuing Connection

One common mistake we make is talking to everyone as though they were our spouses, which can come across as irritating or patronizing. Given the amount of time we spend with our partners, it's natural that they dominate our thoughts and conversations. However, this can lead to deprioritizing others, including our children. Imagine coming home, turning on the TV or computer, and ignoring your partner or displaying disinterest while chatting with colleagues. Such behavior would cause a rift in any relationship. Similarly, our children need to feel valued and appreciated. Communicating from the heart strengthens these bonds and helps relationships flourish.

The Importance of Communication

For centuries, effective communication has been closely linked to success. How we interact with others is essential for developing friendships, attracting a mate, finding and maintaining work, and achieving self-fulfillment. However, as parents and busy individuals, we often find that the demands of life take a toll on our communication skills and our connections with those we care most deeply about. It's crucial to stop, be present, and notice our actions and reactions to ensure all our communications at home and at work are sincere and truthful.

Practical Techniques for Improved Communication

1. **Active Listening**: Give your full attention to your child when they speak. Show interest through eye contact, nodding, and verbal affirmations like "I understand" or "Tell me more." This not only validates their feelings but also builds trust and openness.

2. **Empathy and Understanding**: Put yourself in your child's shoes. Try to understand their perspective and respond with empathy. Acknowledge their feelings and offer support, helping them feel heard and valued.

3. **Non-Verbal Communication**: Pay attention to your body language, facial expressions, and tone of voice. These non-verbal cues can convey as much, if not more, than words. Ensure your non-verbal communication matches your verbal messages to avoid confusion.

4. **Set Aside Quality Time**: Make time for regular one-on-one interactions with your child. Whether it's during a meal, a bedtime routine, or a shared activity, this dedicated time strengthens your bond and fosters open communication.

5. **Positive Reinforcement**: Praise your child's efforts and accomplishments. Positive reinforcement encourages good behavior and boosts their confidence. It also creates a positive communication environment where your child feels appreciated.

6. **Clear and Consistent Messages**: Ensure your messages are clear and consistent. Avoid mixed signals by aligning your

words with your actions. Consistency helps children understand expectations and reduces confusion.

7. **Open-Ended Questions**: Ask open-ended questions that encourage your child to express themselves. Instead of yes/no
questions, try "What was the best part of your day?" or "How
did that make you feel?" This promotes deeper conversations
and critical thinking.

8. **Model Good Communication**: Demonstrate good communication skills through your actions. Show respect, patience,
and active listening in your interactions. Children learn by observing, and your behavior sets a powerful example.

By incorporating these techniques into your daily interactions,
you can enhance communication with your children, creating a nurturing and supportive environment that fosters their emotional and
social development.

CHAPTER 11

Strengthening the Parent-Child Bond

The Importance of Secure Attachment

A recent study of 30-36 month-old children revealed that those with the highest secure attachments from birth to 24 months showed significant advantages in linguistic and cognitive dimensions. Securely attached children surpassed their insecurely attached peers in early learning and cognitive domains by the equivalent of a six-month age advantage. This finding underscores the critical role of secure attachment in a child's ability to thrive, operating within a limited window of time.

The biological imperative for survival necessitated early development in human evolution to ensure "getting started out right." The importance of this early mutual connection is embedded in humans by natural selection over hundreds of thousands of years and is evident in the rapid development of human babies compared to other species. Creating secure attachments is a naturally achieved goal, fostering a state of harmonious bonding, living in the present moment, and extending into a mindfulness practice in loving kindness (Metta).

Building Secure Attachment

To form a secure attachment relationship with our vulnerable children, we need to be attuned to their needs and communicate love and security through all available channels. Their development hinges on our ability to provide "loving, responsive care," which is also crucial for our own happiness and well-being. Spontaneous feelings and direct physical connections often compete fiercely with the demands and rational expectations of life, but both connection and respect for safety are equally necessary. Mother and child are intricately intertwined in this process.

Practical Steps to Strengthen the Parent-Child Bond

1. **Responsive Parenting**: Respond promptly and sensitively to your child's needs. Whether it's feeding, changing, or comforting, being responsive helps build trust and security.
2. **Quality Time**: Spend uninterrupted time with your child. Engage in activities they enjoy and show genuine interest in their experiences and feelings.
3. **Positive Touch**: Physical affection, such as hugs, cuddles, and gentle touch, fosters a sense of security and strengthens the emotional bond between you and your child.
4. **Consistent Routines**: Establishing consistent daily routines provides a sense of stability and predictability, which is crucial for building secure attachments.
5. **Mindful Presence**: Practice being fully present during interactions with your child. This mindfulness enhances your connection and allows you to respond to their needs more effectively.
6. **Empathy and Validation**: Acknowledge and validate your child's emotions. Showing empathy helps them feel understood and valued, which strengthens the parent-child bond.

7. **Encouragement and Support**: Encourage your child's efforts and support their endeavors. Positive reinforcement builds their confidence and reinforces your loving connection.

8. **Open Communication**: Foster open and honest communication. Listen actively to your child and create a safe space for them to express their thoughts and feelings.

By incorporating these practices into your daily routine, you can strengthen the parent-child bond, creating a secure foundation for your child's emotional and cognitive development.

CHAPTER 12

Practicing Mindful Discipline

Rethinking Discipline
Discipline encompasses much more than addressing criminal or antisocial behavior. Unfortunately, our colloquial interpretation often limits our understanding of this essential parenting tool. This narrow view causes us to focus excessively on punishment, attempting to shape our child's sense of self to align with our value system. Other times, we lean heavily on education, using our adult perspective to guide our children toward better choices. However, it's crucial to remember that, in many respects, our children possess a natural enlightenment.

When you discipline mindfully, you create space for your child's development and encourage them to begin a process of self-examination. Mindfulness aids you in observing discipline as an act of love. It helps you step back from preconceptions and biases, allowing you to remain mindful of the countless small lessons imparted through daily interactions. By practicing mindful discipline, you teach your child in the most loving, natural, and meaningful way.

The Role of Discipline in Parenting

Discipline is one of the most powerful expressions of love available to parents. It is a vital tool for helping your child learn and grow. However, discipline can often become a flashpoint in families. Many mothers feel obligated to discipline their children but struggle with how to do so without harming the relationship or the child's developing spirit. In their desire to avoid punishment, parents sometimes use discipline to suppress children's natural impulses – to sit still, walk, talk, draw, or express themselves in noisy, messy, and lively ways.

Children are inherently strong and well-meaning. They have an innate understanding of how they should behave but need time to practice and grow before fully reaching their potential. When children make mistakes, a gentle manner and loving guidance are far more effective in guiding them toward moral and ethical behavior than punishment and righteous fury.

Practical Steps for Mindful Discipline

1. **Reflect on Intentions**: Before disciplining your child, take a moment to reflect on your intentions. Are you aiming to teach and guide, or are you reacting out of frustration? Mindful reflection helps ensure that your actions align with your long-term parenting goals.
2. **Stay Calm**: Mindfulness helps you remain calm and composed, even in challenging situations. By staying calm, you can approach discipline with clarity and compassion, making it a constructive experience for your child.
3. **Communicate Clearly**: Use clear and concise language to explain the reasons for the discipline. Help your child understand the impact of their actions and what they can do differently next time.

4. **Focus on Teaching**: View discipline as an opportunity to teach your child valuable life lessons. Instead of focusing on punishment, emphasize the learning experience and how it can help them grow.

5. **Consistency is Key**: Apply discipline consistently to reinforce boundaries and expectations. Consistency helps children understand the consequences of their actions and fosters a sense of security.

6. **Practice Empathy**: Put yourself in your child's shoes and try to understand their perspective. Empathy allows you to connect with your child on a deeper level and respond to their needs with compassion.

7. **Encourage Self-Reflection**: Encourage your child to reflect on their actions and the reasons behind them. This self-reflection fosters self-awareness and personal growth.

8. **Model Desired Behavior**: Children learn by observing their parents. Model the behavior you wish to see in your child, demonstrating self-discipline, patience, and kindness in your daily interactions.

By incorporating these mindful discipline practices into your parenting routine, you can create a nurturing environment that supports your child's emotional and ethical development.

CHAPTER 13

Promoting Mindful Eating

Choose Habits to Cultivate and Release
Mindful eating begins with choosing which habits to cultivate and which to let go of. Identify one mealtime or snacktime habit to release and one to nurture. For instance, you might decide to stop eating in front of the television or while on the go. Instead, commit to sitting down at a kitchen table for meals and only consuming "grab-and-go" foods when you're actually on the move, rather than making a meal and rushing out the door.

Steps to Begin:

1. **Make a List**: Document instances where you engage in mindless eating. Identify the times and situations where this happens most frequently.
2. **Evaluate Habits**: Determine which habits you'd like to release and which ones you want to cultivate. This reflection helps you create intentional and mindful eating practices.

Understand Your Historical Relationship with Food

Reflecting on your past experiences with food can offer valuable insights into your current eating habits. Consider what foods you were drawn to and why. Are there specific memories tied to certain foods that make them "good" or "bad" in your mind? Think about your social interactions around food while growing up. How did family members describe different dishes to you, whether for breakfast, school, work, holidays, or regular days? Did you grow up with parents or caregivers who insisted you finish your plate regardless of feeling full?

Questions to Ponder:

1. **Food Memories**: What positive or negative memories do you associate with specific foods?
2. **Family Influence**: How did your family's attitudes and behaviors around food shape your own eating habits?
3. **Emotional Eating**: Notice how your history with food influences your current eating patterns, especially in emotional or stressful situations.

Clarify Your Intention Surrounding Food

Establishing a clear intention for your meals is crucial for mindful eating. Reflect on what you aim to achieve with your eating habits. Are you looking to nourish yourself and your family with healthy food? Do you want to raise children who are not picky eaters? Choose a primary intention around the role of food in your life.

Steps to Clarify Intention:

1. **Define Your Goals**: Outline your main goals for yourself and your family regarding food and nutrition.

2. **Set Intentions**: Clearly state your intention, such as "I want to nourish my body with healthy foods" or "I aim to create a positive and enjoyable mealtime environment for my family."
3. **Regular Reflection**: Regularly revisit this intention to keep your mindful eating habits aligned with your goals.

Practical Exercises for Mindful Eating

1. **Mindful Eating Rituals**: Create rituals around mealtime that encourage mindfulness. This could include setting the table, expressing gratitude before eating, or taking a few deep breaths to center yourself before starting a meal.
2. **Savor Each Bite**: Take the time to savor each bite of food. Pay attention to the flavors, textures, and aromas. Eating slowly and mindfully can enhance your enjoyment and prevent overeating.
3. **Avoid Distractions**: Minimize distractions such as TV, phones, or computers during meals. Focus solely on the act of eating and the company you are with.
4. **Portion Awareness**: Be mindful of portion sizes and listen to your body's hunger and fullness cues. Serve reasonable portions and avoid the pressure to finish everything on your plate.
5. **Emotional Check-In**: Before reaching for food, check in with your emotions. Are you truly hungry, or are you eating out of boredom, stress, or habit? Address emotional needs in ways other than eating.
6. **Engage All Senses**: Engage all your senses in the eating experience. Notice the colors, smells, and textures of your food. This practice enhances your connection to the meal and promotes mindful eating.

By integrating these practices into your daily routine, you can cultivate a healthier and more mindful relationship with food, benefiting both yourself and your family.

CHAPTER 14

Creating Mindful Rituals and Routines

Embracing Mindfulness Amidst Motherhood
As I have embraced mindfulness, I've noticed a significant shift in my patience and spare time, especially after becoming a mother. Initially, I felt overwhelmed and had little interest in adding more to my plate. However, I've discovered that incorporating simple, mindfulness-based activities into my daily life has subtly yet profoundly opened up new ways of being present. These activities, though modest, serve as a sanctuary amidst the chaos of sleep deprivation and time constraints.

Despite the seeming impossibility of establishing rituals as a mother, these practices have been my anchor through the transition into motherhood. For generations, women have upheld traditions and routines that provide a sense of grounding and continuity. Similarly, mindfulness has become an essential part of my daily life, not just as a solitary exercise but particularly enduring when I am with my children.

The Power of Simple Mindfulness Practices
Over the years, mindfulness has become integral to my life, guiding me through the random, yet precious, moments of each day. I

practice meditation and various yogic techniques, ensuring that I am present and attentive. These practices are not about achieving perfection but about finding strength and clarity amidst the demands of motherhood.

Invisible Practices for New Moms:

1. **Mindful Breathing**: Take a few moments to focus on your breath. This simple act can be done anywhere and helps center your mind.
2. **Gratitude Journaling**: Write down a few things you are grateful for each day. This practice shifts your focus to positive aspects of your life.
3. **Mindful Walking**: During walks with your child, pay attention to your surroundings. Notice the colors, sounds, and sensations, grounding yourself in the present moment.
4. **Mini Meditations**: Incorporate short meditation sessions into your day. Even five minutes of mindful meditation can bring a sense of calm and clarity.

Establishing Rituals for Consistency and Stability

While the idea of rituals may seem unrealistic, they can provide much-needed consistency and stability. Mindfulness, woven into the fabric of daily life, offers a grounding force. It is not just an unsocial exercise but a practice that strengthens your bond with your children and enriches your interactions.

Mindful Routines to Practice:

1. **Morning Meditation**: Start your day with a few minutes of meditation. Set an intention for the day and carry this mindfulness into your interactions.

2. **Mindful Mealtime**: Use mealtime as an opportunity to practice mindfulness. Engage with your children, savor the food, and express gratitude.

3. **Bedtime Rituals**: Establish calming bedtime rituals, such as reading a book together or practicing deep breathing. These routines help create a sense of security and relaxation.

4. **Weekly Reflection**: Take time each week to reflect on your experiences and intentions. This practice helps you stay connected to your inner self and your goals as a parent.

Strengthening Through Mindfulness

Mindfulness allows me to approach motherhood with a sense of strength and clarity. I remind myself not to demand perfection from my children, knowing that they are on their own journey of growth and learning. By being mindful, I become more independent of my emotional reactions, fostering a healthier and more supportive environment for my family. This mindful approach protects our valuable time together, ensuring that we move forward with understanding and compassion.

CHAPTER 15

Balancing Work and Family Life

Defining Family Time

One of the first steps in balancing work and family life is to define and prioritize family time. Engage in conversations with your children about what they would like to do together. Establish specific days and routines that create a sense of rhythm and stability. For example, you might have "Sweet Tuesday," "Perfect Wednesday," or "4-Hour Friday," with structured activities like breakfast, homework, piano, playtime, reading, and bedtime. Ensure that these times are free from distractions, such as phones or televisions, to foster genuine connection.

By creating a "honeycomb time" approach, you can work bee-style in your family hive, with rules that help the hive flourish. Work must be done during designated work times, and once completed, it is time for play or quiet activities. This structured yet flexible routine ensures that each family member's needs are met, making your collective energy and time richer.

The Myth of Perfect Balance

Finding balance is an ongoing process and often feels like a pipe dream. It is important to acknowledge that pleasing everyone all the time is impossible. When faced with competing demands from work and family, ask yourself, "What will actually happen if I don't get this done?" or "What will I miss if I don't take this time for myself or my family?" It is essential to allow for some risk in this balance, as avoiding it altogether sets you up for failure.

Embracing Imperfection

Accepting that failure is simply a step toward success is a key aspect of balancing work and family life. A wise woman finds happiness despite knowing this. Learning to live in the face of the unknown and embracing the rise and fall of every tide brings real peace. This balance is not about eliminating chaos but about finding ways to navigate it without being overwhelmed.

Practical Tips for Balancing Work and Family

1. **Set Clear Boundaries**: Define clear boundaries between work and family time. Communicate these boundaries with your employer and colleagues, ensuring that family time is respected.

2. **Prioritize Tasks**: Focus on the most important tasks at work and home. Use tools like to-do lists and time management apps to stay organized and ensure you are addressing high-priority items.

3. **Delegate Responsibilities**: Share household responsibilities with your partner and children. Delegating tasks not only lightens your load but also teaches children valuable life skills.

4. **Embrace Flexibility**: Be flexible with your schedule. There will be times when work demands more of your attention and times when family needs take precedence. Adaptability is key to maintaining balance.

5. **Practice Self-Care**: Take care of your physical and mental well-being. Schedule regular self-care activities, such as exercise, meditation, or hobbies, to recharge and stay resilient.

6. **Use Technology Wisely**: Leverage technology to streamline work tasks and stay connected with family. However, also set boundaries for screen time to ensure quality, distraction-free interactions with your loved ones.

7. **Reflect and Adjust**: Regularly reflect on your work-life balance and make adjustments as needed. What worked last month may not work now, so stay open to changes and continuously seek improvement.

Cultivating Peace Amidst Chaos

Balancing work and family life is about finding peace amidst the chaos. It involves living in harmony with the ebb and flow of life's demands and learning the power to thrive despite tumultuous times. By setting realistic expectations, embracing imperfection, and prioritizing what truly matters, you can create a balanced, fulfilling life for yourself and your family.

CHAPTER 16

Fostering Mindful Relationships

The Role of Parental Communication

Much of the tension and animosity within a family often stems from the parents' communication styles. When parents fail to exhibit empathy, family members may become dismissive and hostile toward one another. This behavior paves the way for emotional detachment and isolation, leaving family members in a constant state of emotional upheaval. A practical antidote to this issue is cultivating a culture that nurtures trust and empathy by "heightening self-awareness." By becoming more self-aware, parents can better assess and reflect on their demeanor during interactions, thereby fostering a more harmonious family environment.

The Beauty of Mindfulness in Relationships

One of the most beautiful aspects of mindfulness is its potential to foster attachment, mutual respect, and empathy within our relationships. As your children grow and develop, they learn by observing you. Your demeanor with them and others provides the most effective instruction. By practicing mindfulness daily, you help teach your children how to navigate the world with peace, infusing your relationships with kindness, respect, and compassion.

Congratulations! Every mindful moment you cultivate contributes significantly to healthy, positive attitudes and behaviors within your family. By being a mindful parent, you are making strides as both a mother and an individual.

Practical Steps for Fostering Mindful Relationships

1. **Practice Active Listening**: Engage in active listening by giving your full attention when a family member speaks. Show empathy and understanding, and avoid interrupting or judging.
2. **Communicate with Empathy**: Approach conversations with empathy and compassion. Acknowledge the feelings and perspectives of others, and respond thoughtfully.
3. **Model Positive Behavior**: Children learn by observing their parents. Model the behavior you wish to see in your children, such as patience, kindness, and respect.
4. **Create Shared Rituals**: Establish family rituals that promote connection and mindfulness. These could include shared meals, family meetings, or regular activities that everyone enjoys.
5. **Practice Self-Awareness**: Reflect on your own emotions and reactions. By understanding your triggers and responses, you can approach interactions with greater clarity and mindfulness.
6. **Encourage Open Communication**: Foster an environment where family members feel comfortable expressing their thoughts and feelings. Encourage honesty and openness in all interactions.
7. **Show Appreciation**: Regularly express gratitude and appreciation for your family members. Acknowledging their efforts

and contributions strengthens your bond and fosters positive relationships.

8. **Resolve Conflicts Mindfully**: Approach conflicts with a calm and open mind. Focus on understanding the root cause of the issue and work together to find a resolution that respects everyone's needs.

By incorporating these practices into your daily interactions, you can foster mindful relationships that are based on trust, empathy, and mutual respect. These efforts will not only enhance the well-being of your family but also create a nurturing environment where everyone can thrive.

Embracing Imperfection and Letting Go of Guilt

The Essence of Mindfulness

When we meditate or practice mindfulness, we are not striving to achieve any specific emotional state or thought. Instead, the practice is about being present in each moment, opening ourselves to our experiences. By fully embracing both joy and sadness, softening our resistance to discomfort, and letting go of striving, we begin a conscious dialogue with ourselves and our practice. This awareness gradually integrates into our daily lives. Whether preparing dinner, writing a blog post, or mothering, we find moments of peace when we immerse ourselves in each step, savoring the process as much as the end result.

Embracing Chaos in Mindfulness Practice

In some ways, the therapeutic setting of a mindfulness group is an exercise in embracing chaos. The unpredictability of small children during a session creates a noisy, chaotic atmosphere. However, amidst this chaos, mothers practice being present in real time, paying attention to their direct experiences even when faced with crying babies, running toddlers, and various stressors. This is the goal of mothers practicing mindfulness: to fully inhabit ourselves, even amid the stressors and joys that come with mothering.

Ironically, many people seek my guidance as a therapist and mommy guru because they are striving for perfection. However, the actual journey is about embracing imperfection in what we can and cannot control.

The Journey of Embracing Imperfection

1. **Acceptance**: Accept that perfection is an unrealistic goal. Understand that imperfection is a natural part of life and parenting. This acceptance allows you to release the pressure of always striving to be perfect.
2. **Self-Compassion**: Practice self-compassion by being kind to yourself when things don't go as planned. Acknowledge your efforts and celebrate your progress rather than focusing on your perceived shortcomings.
3. **Letting Go of Guilt**: Guilt often arises from unrealistic expectations and self-imposed pressures. Let go of guilt by recognizing that you are doing your best with the resources available to you. Guilt does not serve you or your family.
4. **Mindful Presence**: Focus on being present in each moment, whether joyful or challenging. Embrace the process rather than fixating on the outcome. This presence helps you find peace in the midst of chaos.
5. **Realistic Expectations**: Set realistic expectations for yourself and your children. Understand that mistakes and setbacks are part of the learning and growth process for both you and your children.
6. **Celebrate Small Wins**: Celebrate the small victories and milestones along the way. Acknowledge the progress you and your children make, no matter how minor it may seem.

7. **Practice Gratitude**: Cultivate gratitude for the experiences and lessons that imperfection brings. Gratitude shifts your focus from what is lacking to what is present and valuable in your life.

Embracing the Full Spectrum of Motherhood

By embracing imperfection, you learn to inhabit yourself fully, experiencing the full spectrum of emotions that come with motherhood. This practice allows you to navigate the joys and challenges with greater ease and resilience. Embracing imperfection also sets a powerful example for your children, teaching them to accept themselves and others without judgment.

CHAPTER 18

Mindfulness for Sleep and Rest

Embracing Stillness and Silence
In the final months of pregnancy, incorporating mindfulness practices can significantly support sleep and lactation. Guided walking meditations and self-massage techniques are beneficial for promoting relaxation. Additionally, guided sitting and standing meditations can help you explore the positive effects of stillness and silence, such as connecting with your baby's heartbeat.

Key Practices:

- **Walking Meditation**: Incorporate walking meditation into your daily routine. Focus on the sensation of each step, the rhythm of your breathing, and the connection with nature. This practice not only supports mindfulness but also aids in gentle physical activity.
- **Self-Massage**: Practice self-massage techniques to promote relaxation and support lactation. Focus on gentle, soothing movements that help release tension and foster a sense of calm.

Cultivating Mindfulness with Intention

As you prepare for the arrival of your baby, it's important to practice mindfulness with intention. Learn to skillfully shift your perspective and attention to include the needs of your growing baby. Move slowly and deliberately, allowing these mindfulness skills to support your rest without forcing yourself to constantly adapt.

Tips for Intentional Mindfulness:

- **Separate Experiences**: Keep the elements of your experience in separate containers. This means cultivating mindfulness with intention and being present in each moment without merging different experiences.
- **Move Slowly**: Allow yourself to move slowly and mindfully. This deliberate pace helps you integrate mindfulness practices into your daily routine, supporting restful sleep and relaxation.

Relaxation Techniques

All the exercises in Part II include components that imitate sleep and rest. This section begins by breaking down the concept of relaxation and includes a yoga exercise that features a forward bend. For this posture, you'll need to lift your feet and sit on a block. This mild variation gives the pregnant body plenty of space to move and helps maintain a strong, steady base for safe positioning.

Yoga and Breathing Techniques:

- **Forward Bend**: Practice forward bends with modifications suitable for pregnancy. This posture helps create space in your body and supports relaxation.
- **Relaxed Breathing**: Learn to relax your breathing rhythm while standing with your feet hip-width apart. This technique

helps you find calm and stability, even if you're accustomed to different warm-up exercises in your routine.

Creating a Restful Environment

Creating a restful environment is crucial for promoting sleep and relaxation. Focus on establishing routines and spaces that encourage calmness and tranquility.

Practical Steps for a Restful Environment:

1. **Sleep Hygiene**: Maintain good sleep hygiene by setting a regular bedtime, creating a comfortable sleep environment, and minimizing screen time before bed.
2. **Calming Rituals**: Incorporate calming rituals into your nighttime routine. This could include a warm bath, reading a book, or practicing gentle yoga.
3. **Mindful Breathing**: Practice mindful breathing exercises before bed. Focus on deep, slow breaths to help quiet your mind and prepare your body for sleep.

By integrating these mindfulness practices into your daily routine, you can support restful sleep and relaxation, creating a nurturing environment for both yourself and your baby.

CHAPTER 19

Mindful Self-Care Practices

The Importance of Self-Care

Remember that you are worth taking care of. Prioritizing your own well-being is fundamental to being able to approach everything else with love, devotion, and pleasure. By taking even five minutes daily for self-care, you lay the foundation for a healthier, more balanced life. Here are some favorite self-care habits to honor yourself with:

Favorite Self-Care Habits

1. **Touch and Massage**: Incorporate regular touch and massage into your routine. For instance, during a DETOX course, I recommended a daily honey massage before bathing. This practice not only soothes your body but also nourishes your skin and promotes relaxation.
2. **Movement**: Ensure you move your body daily. This could be as simple as practicing gratitude for the ability to walk or take care of your children. Physical movement helps release tension, boosts your mood, and enhances overall well-being.

3. **Quality Alone Time**: Allocate quality time for yourself. We can only give to others when we have enough for ourselves. Taking a week where my husband bathed the children and handled after-dinner routines allowed me to regain my energy and focus.

The Essential Nature of Self-Care for Mothers

Mindful self-care practices are absolutely essential for mothers. By putting self-care at the top of our list, we model healthy attitudes around self-love and worthiness for our children. This is an incredibly valuable gift that mothers can give to their children. You cannot take care of another person if you are not taking good care of yourself. If you do not consider your own well-being as essential, burnout becomes inevitable.

As mothers, we often have more tasks on our plates than what time and energy allow us to accomplish. Constant self-criticism and the belief that we are not good enough or unworthy of even five minutes for ourselves – something that costs no money – can lead to immense suffering, stress, and burnout. It is our responsibility to demonstrate a balanced and well-cared-for life for our children, modeling the way to a healthier, happier life.

Practical Self-Care Tips

1. **Daily Rituals**: Establish daily self-care rituals, such as a morning stretch, a mindful cup of tea, or a bedtime gratitude practice. These small acts can significantly impact your well-being.
2. **Healthy Boundaries**: Set boundaries to protect your time and energy. This includes saying no to additional responsibilities that can overwhelm you and carving out time for self-care.

3. **Nourishing Activities**: Engage in activities that nourish your mind, body, and soul. This could be reading, gardening, painting, or taking a nature walk. Choose activities that bring you joy and relaxation.

4. **Mindful Breathing**: Practice mindful breathing exercises to center yourself and reduce stress. Even a few minutes of deep, focused breathing can calm your mind and rejuvenate your spirit.

5. **Connect with Loved Ones**: Maintain connections with friends and family who support and uplift you. Sharing your experiences and feelings with others can provide emotional relief and strengthen your support network.

6. **Seek Professional Support**: If you find it challenging to manage stress and self-care on your own, consider seeking professional support from a therapist or counselor. They can offer valuable insights and strategies tailored to your needs.

By integrating these mindful self-care practices into your daily routine, you can create a healthier, more balanced life for yourself and your family.

CHAPTER 20

Mindfulness in Moments of Chaos and Overwhelm

Navigating the Unknowns with a New Baby
There are always unknowns with a new baby, and unexpected chaos can be incredibly unsettling for many parents. Preparing for worst-case scenarios in advance, much like keeping winter coats or an emergency evacuation bag handy, can serve as a security blanket. This "what if" disaster planning helps you feel more prepared to navigate potential crises alone.

Mindfulness, proven to boost problem-solving skills, focus, and a sense of well-being, can be invaluable in overcoming anxious states. It helped me during the night when I was recovering from the shock of a failed epidural amidst the chaos of our late preterm son's birth.

Real-Life Examples of Mindfulness in Parenting

Patrick Ormond, an actor and real estate agent, and a single parent to "four under four and a half with my Irish twins," shares how mindfulness taught him to be present and reduce his chaotic state. "I learned to keep my cup full so I could be a better father every day. It was the lessons I learned on the cushion that enabled me to navigate the chaos with some level of grace," he said.

For mothers on solo duty moment to moment, grace means giving yourself permission to step back when needed and even leave if necessary. It is physically and mentally impossible to be everywhere with multiple young children hitting their meltdowns simultaneously, especially when doing it alone. **Christina Britt**, a Windsor, Ontario-based mind-body physiologist and yoga teacher, emphasizes, "I can't physically hold them all or tend to the universal upset that has suddenly popped up. Whether they are smooth or loud, I must allow them to have their feelings."

Practical Steps for Mindfulness in Chaos

1. **Prepare Mentally**: Think through potential scenarios and how you might handle them. This mental rehearsal helps you feel more prepared and reduces anxiety.
2. **Stay Present**: Focus on the present moment rather than worrying about the future or dwelling on the past. Mindfulness practices like deep breathing or grounding exercises can help you stay centered.
3. **Embrace Imperfection**: Accept that you cannot control everything and that it's okay to step back or take a break when needed. Embrace the chaos as part of the parenting journey.
4. **Allow Emotions**: Allow your children to express their feelings, whether they are smooth or loud. Acknowledge their emotions and provide a safe space for them to process their experiences.
5. **Practice Self-Compassion**: Be kind to yourself during stressful moments. Recognize that you are doing your best and that it's okay to seek support or take a moment for yourself.
6. **Create a Calming Environment**: Establish routines and spaces that promote calmness. This might include a quiet corner for meditation or a soothing playlist for stressful times.

7. **Seek Support**: Don't hesitate to reach out for help from friends, family, or professionals. Sharing the load can make a significant difference in managing chaos and overwhelm.

By incorporating these mindfulness practices into your daily life, you can navigate moments of chaos and overwhelm with greater ease and resilience, creating a more balanced and harmonious environment for yourself and your family.

CHAPTER 21

Mindfulness for Pregnancy and Postpartum

Navigating the Unknown with Mindfulness
Pregnancy and postpartum periods are filled with unknowns, making them inherently challenging. However, if we can become mindful and open in these moments of uncertainty, suspending judgment and uncovering empathy, the context of our child's birth and our early days together can be nourishing, nurturing, and secure. Mindfulness practices can strengthen and support both mothers and fathers, helping them navigate both positive outcomes and difficult moments, such as medical complications or intense stress.

Embracing Mindfulness During Pregnancy
Pregnancy requires a heightened level of mindfulness, as it often compels women to be open to potential risks and uncertainties. This period initiates parents into a realm where they must continually open themselves to the body's experiences, their partner's experiences, and the unknown demands of the future. The physical and emotional context into which a baby arrives—such as the home environment, neighborhood, and relational histories—has a profound

impact on the baby's development. These intricate layers of context influence the formation of the baby's personality and brain development in ways that are often beyond our understanding.

Practical Mindfulness Practices for Pregnancy and Postpartum

1. **Mindful Breathing**: Practice deep, mindful breathing to center yourself and reduce stress. Focus on the rhythm of your breath, allowing it to bring calmness and clarity.
2. **Body Scan Meditation**: Use body scan meditation to connect with your body and identify areas of tension. This practice helps you become more attuned to your physical sensations and promotes relaxation.
3. **Journaling**: Keep a journal to express your thoughts and emotions. Reflecting on your experiences can provide insight and help you process the challenges and joys of pregnancy and postpartum.
4. **Gratitude Practice**: Cultivate a sense of gratitude by acknowledging the positive aspects of your journey. Write down things you are grateful for each day, fostering a positive mindset.
5. **Support Networks**: Engage with support networks, such as prenatal and postpartum groups, to share experiences and receive emotional support. Connecting with others who are going through similar experiences can be incredibly reassuring.
6. **Gentle Yoga**: Incorporate gentle yoga into your routine to promote physical well-being and relaxation. Prenatal yoga classes can provide safe and effective exercises tailored to your needs.
7. **Mindful Eating**: Practice mindful eating by paying attention to the taste, texture, and aroma of your food. This practice can

help you make healthier food choices and enjoy your meals more fully.

Integrating Mindfulness into Parenting

As you transition into parenthood, mindfulness can continue to play a vital role. By being present and open, you can navigate the demands and uncertainties of parenting with greater ease. Mindfulness helps you remain calm and focused, enabling you to respond to your baby's needs with compassion and clarity.

Tips for Mindful Parenting:

- **Stay Present**: Focus on being fully present during interactions with your baby. Pay attention to their cues and respond with empathy.
- **Practice Patience**: Cultivate patience by recognizing that both you and your baby are learning and growing together. Allow yourself grace during challenging moments.
- **Self-Compassion**: Be kind to yourself and acknowledge the effort you are putting into parenting. Self-compassion fosters a positive and nurturing environment for both you and your baby.

By integrating mindfulness practices into your daily routine, you can create a nurturing and supportive environment for yourself and your family, fostering a sense of well-being and connection during pregnancy and postpartum.

CHAPTER 22

Mindfulness and the Teenage Years

The Superpower of Mindful Parenting

Practicing mindfulness with your children, especially during their difficult and fragile teenage years, can feel like a superpower. Mums who are fully present with their kids develop an incessant, almost supernatural patience. It's a day-by-day learning process, but the closer we approach actions with mindfulness, the better we support our children's growth. When a mum is mindful in everything she does, she achieves an incredible resolve, making her seemingly invincible to the chaos, noise, and intensity of parenting teens.

Mindfulness is a superpower that grows with each mindful moment, transforming small opportunities into powerful expressions of calm and resilience. It's important to keep the fire of mindfulness burning, even in moments of lost passion, staying aware of the next potential mindful moment. This lifelong tender care blossoms, even through the challenging teenage years.

Observing Mindful Parents

Living on a tiny island, I often encounter some of the most mindful mums and dads and their teenage children. Whether on the streets, at home, in the supermarket, or at cafes, I observe a distinct difference in how these mindful parents communicate with their children. Their interactions often evoke envy from onlookers, as the parents and children exhibit mutual respect, empathy, and understanding.

Embracing Reality

However, it's important to dispel the misconception that mindfulness leads to a perfect relationship or a peaceful, perfect home. Real life is not always serene, and every family faces challenges. Mindfulness helps navigate these challenges with grace, but it does not eliminate them.

Practical Steps for Mindful Parenting with Teens

1. **Active Listening**: Engage in active listening with your teenagers. Give them your full attention, acknowledge their feelings, and respond with empathy. This builds trust and strengthens your relationship.
2. **Modeling Behavior**: Demonstrate the behaviors you wish to see in your teens. Whether it's patience, respect, or open communication, modeling these behaviors encourages your children to adopt them.
3. **Setting Boundaries**: Establish clear and consistent boundaries. Boundaries provide a sense of security and help teens understand expectations. Be firm but fair, and involve your teens in setting these boundaries.
4. **Encouraging Independence**: Support your teens' growing independence by giving them opportunities to make decisions and learn from their mistakes. This fosters a sense of responsibility and self-confidence.
5. **Quality Time**: Spend quality time together, engaging in activities that your teen enjoys. This helps strengthen your bond and creates positive shared experiences.

6. **Mindful Conflict Resolution**: Approach conflicts with a calm and open mind. Focus on understanding the root cause of the issue and work together to find a solution that respects everyone's needs.

7. **Self-Compassion**: Practice self-compassion and allow yourself to make mistakes. Parenting teens is challenging, and it's important to be kind to yourself and recognize your efforts.

8. **Open Communication**: Foster an environment where open communication is encouraged. Create a safe space for your teens to express their thoughts and feelings without fear of judgment.

By incorporating these mindfulness practices into your parenting routine, you can navigate the teenage years with greater ease and resilience, fostering a nurturing and supportive environment for your family.

CHAPTER 23

Mindfulness as a Tool for Resilience

Dismantling Emotional Barriers

Mindfulness practice helps us dismantle the walls that block us from accessing our natural wellspring of loving-kindness. It enables us to recognize and release the conditioning that imprisons us in harmful reactivity and shameful beliefs. By doing so, we become better equipped to respond to our families' needs rather than reacting reflexively. Mindfulness is not solely about shedding the burden of habitual fear and conditioning; it also opens the door to peace, spaciousness, attentiveness, creativity, and, most importantly, love.

Love pours naturally from an open heart and is the greatest force for good we can offer our children and the world. Being mindful with them lays a key foundation for this growth. This is the gift of mindfulness practice: the capacity to heal, grow, and share love among parents, children, family, friends, society, and humanity.

The Relationship with Yourself

Behind your relationship with your children lies your relationship with yourself. How we see ourselves dictates how we see our children—whether we view them as a source of well-being to be cherished and cultivated or a source of suffering to be resisted or changed. Unfortunately, the beliefs we hold about ourselves often reflect the painful messages we have received about our acceptability. These detrimental beliefs are the bricks that weigh down our hearts and create distance between us and our families.

In stressful moments, these beliefs heighten our reactivity and decrease our ability to act with creativity and love. We respond according to habit and history, saying or doing something destructive, and then our hearts sink. Mindfulness can help us break this cycle.

Building Resilience Through Mindfulness

1. **Self-Awareness**: Mindfulness enhances self-awareness, helping us recognize and understand our emotional triggers. By being aware of these triggers, we can respond thoughtfully rather than react impulsively.

2. **Emotional Regulation**: Regular mindfulness practice strengthens our ability to regulate emotions. We learn to navigate intense feelings with greater ease, reducing the likelihood of destructive responses.

3. **Empathy and Compassion**: Mindfulness fosters empathy and compassion, both for ourselves and others. This empathetic mindset allows us to connect more deeply with our children and respond to their needs with love and understanding.

4. **Positive Self-Perception**: Through mindfulness, we can shift our self-perception from one based on harmful beliefs to one grounded in acceptance and love. This positive self-view enhances our ability to enjoy and celebrate our children as they are.

5. **Stress Reduction**: Mindfulness reduces stress by promoting relaxation and a sense of inner peace. By managing stress ef-

fectively, we can approach parenting with a calm and centered demeanor.

6. **Creative Problem-Solving**: A mindful approach enhances our ability to think creatively and solve problems. This flexibility is crucial for navigating the challenges of parenting with resilience and grace.

Practical Mindfulness Practices for Building Resilience

1. **Mindful Breathing**: Practice mindful breathing to center yourself and calm your mind. Focus on each breath, allowing it to anchor you in the present moment.

2. **Body Scan Meditation**: Use body scan meditation to connect with your physical sensations and release tension. This practice enhances your awareness of how stress manifests in your body and helps you relax.

3. **Loving-Kindness Meditation**: Engage in loving-kindness meditation to cultivate feelings of compassion and love. Extend these feelings toward yourself, your children, and others in your life.

4. **Mindful Reflection**: Reflect on your interactions with your children. Consider how mindfulness can improve your responses and strengthen your relationships.

5. **Journaling**: Keep a mindfulness journal to document your experiences, insights, and progress. Writing helps solidify your practice and provides a space for self-reflection.

6. **Mindful Activities**: Incorporate mindfulness into daily activities, such as eating, walking, or playing with your children. Focus on being fully present and engaged in these moments.

By integrating mindfulness practices into your daily life, you can build resilience, foster loving relationships, and create a nurturing environment for your family.

CHAPTER 24

Mindfulness for Single Mothers

The Overwhelming Responsibilities

Being a single mother often means shouldering a multitude of responsibilities, both financial and emotional. It began with becoming aware that the task was consuming me, more so than my daughter. Besides the care and its responsibilities, she only needed me to play or listen to her stories. However, I found myself waking at the crack of dawn to work, dashing out of client meetings, and constantly worrying about her safety and well-being. These anxieties took root in my mind, blossoming into thorny doubts that dictated my mood and led to exhaustion and irritability. The year 2016 was spent feeling overwhelmed and depleted, with my energy for my daughter overshadowed by exhaustion that colored our routine with vehemence.

The Reality of Single Motherhood

While I am well-versed in handling tasks solo, I hesitate to call myself a single mother. It's more accurate to describe myself as a "human-woman-orbiting-a-hot-10-1/2-year-old-girl-alone-in-space."
On the internet, single mothers are often portrayed as brave, loving, and impressively organized. However, beneath the props and affir-

mation lies the real struggle: the distress, confusion, and exhaustion that come with being the sole caregiver. This gap between the status and experience is widened by parochial myths and Hollywood glamour, depicting single mothers as overworked, under-slept superheroes weighed down by despair. Despite occasional help from grandparents and a stepmother, I often felt alone with my challenges. Yet, mindfulness has been a crucial tool in improving the daily struggle of single motherhood.

The Power of Mindfulness

Mindfulness helps us dismantle the barriers that block us from accessing our natural wellspring of loving-kindness. It enables us to recognize and release the conditioning that imprisons us in harmful reactivity and shameful beliefs. By being mindful, we can respond to our children's needs rather than reacting reflexively, creating a nurturing environment even in challenging times.

Practical Mindfulness Practices for Single Mothers

1. **Mindful Breathing**: Practice mindful breathing to center yourself and reduce stress. Focus on each breath, allowing it to bring calmness and clarity.
2. **Self-Compassion**: Be kind to yourself and acknowledge the effort you are putting into parenting. Self-compassion fosters a positive and nurturing environment for both you and your child.
3. **Journaling**: Keep a journal to express your thoughts and emotions. Reflecting on your experiences can provide insight and help you process the challenges and joys of single motherhood.
4. **Quality Time**: Spend quality time with your child, engaging in activities that they enjoy. This helps strengthen your bond and creates positive shared experiences.

5. **Support Networks**: Engage with support networks, such as single parent groups or online communities, to share experiences and receive emotional support. Connecting with others who are going through similar experiences can be incredibly reassuring.

6. **Set Realistic Expectations**: Set realistic expectations for yourself and your child. Understand that mistakes and setbacks are part of the learning and growth process for both of you.

7. **Gratitude Practice**: Cultivate a sense of gratitude by acknowledging the positive aspects of your journey. Write down things you are grateful for each day, fostering a positive mindset.

8. **Create a Calming Environment**: Establish routines and spaces that promote calmness. This might include a quiet corner for meditation or a soothing playlist for stressful times.

By integrating these mindfulness practices into your daily routine, you can navigate the challenges of single motherhood with greater ease and resilience, creating a nurturing and supportive environment for yourself and your child.

CHAPTER 25

Mindfulness for Mothers of Children with Special N

Embracing the Reality of Motherhood

Unlike the mother of fiction, the mother of change is multi-dimensional. She is a mature woman who begins to find fulfillment in new areas of her life as her children grow up. She is confident, happy, and takes care of herself. Her preparation for motherhood couldn't prepare her for the actual reality of it. She adores and is befuddled by her little people in equal measure. She has experienced both failure and success and can acknowledge these times for what they are—moments of her life.

Challenging Beliefs and Expectations

It is crucial to explore and challenge our beliefs about who we think we are and who we think we should be as mothers. We may hold stereotypes, unrealistic expectations, or outdated scripts associated with mothering, leading us to judge and police ourselves and others. These ideas and expectations are shaped by various influences throughout our lives, often making us feel the weight of needing to be many things simultaneously.

As mothers, we have the right to claim a sense of ourselves in who we wish to be. By questioning and redefining these roles, we open up the possibility of becoming the mother of change. Who might you become when you let go of these limiting beliefs and embrace your authentic self?

The Struggle for Self-Care

Mothers often struggle to find time for themselves. Engaging in pursuits that make a mother feel alive and connected is essential, but so is finding time alone. For mothers of children with special needs, carving out this time can be particularly challenging. Appreciating self-care looks different for everyone, and for some, it may simply be letting go of the belief that taking time for oneself is selfish.

Practical Mindfulness Practices for Mothers of Children with Special Needs

1. **Mindful Breathing**: Practice mindful breathing to center yourself and reduce stress. Focus on each breath, allowing it to bring calmness and clarity.
2. **Self-Compassion**: Be kind to yourself and acknowledge the effort you are putting into parenting. Self-compassion fosters a positive and nurturing environment for both you and your child.
3. **Journaling**: Keep a journal to express your thoughts and emotions. Reflecting on your experiences can provide insight and help you process the challenges and joys of motherhood.
4. **Quality Time**: Spend quality time with your child, engaging in activities that they enjoy. This helps strengthen your bond and creates positive shared experiences.
5. **Support Networks**: Engage with support networks, such as groups for parents of children with special needs or online communities, to share experiences and receive emotional sup-

port. Connecting with others who understand your journey can be incredibly reassuring.

6. **Set Realistic Expectations**: Set realistic expectations for yourself and your child. Understand that mistakes and setbacks are part of the learning and growth process for both of you.

7. **Gratitude Practice**: Cultivate a sense of gratitude by acknowledging the positive aspects of your journey. Write down things you are grateful for each day, fostering a positive mindset.

8. **Create a Calming Environment**: Establish routines and spaces that promote calmness. This might include a quiet corner for meditation or a soothing playlist for stressful times.

9. **Ask for Help**: Don't hesitate to ask for help from friends, family, or professional caregivers. Having additional support can make a significant difference in managing your responsibilities and maintaining your well-being.

10. **Engage in Activities You Love**: Make time for activities that bring you joy and fulfillment, whether it's a hobby, exercise, or simply taking a walk in nature.

By integrating these mindfulness practices into your daily routine, you can navigate the unique challenges of raising a child with special needs with greater ease and resilience, creating a nurturing and supportive environment for yourself and your family.

CHAPTER 26

Mindfulness and Parenting Styles

The Role of Mindfulness in Parenting

Mindfulness in parenting is about being present and making conscious choices moment to moment. It's especially crucial in challenging situations, where our children's behavior can trigger strong emotional reactions. By focusing on our breath and softening it in these moments, we create a space to respond thoughtfully rather than react impulsively. This approach helps bridge the gap between our reactive tendencies and the calm, non-coercive parent we strive to be.

A Personal Example

Earlier, when looking into panic-driven eyes, I turned to my breath, albeit too little too late, and managed to slightly soften my voice. I realized that my daughter's cultural immaturity, similar to her brother's, is very frustrating to most observers of her behavior. Being a mother and teaching grounding to others has given me the awareness over time to detect the bridge between the woman who hurls objects when she gets too trigger-happy and the calm and non-coercive mother.

At the Arboretum, I found myself raising my voice as my 7-year-old daughter refused to leave long after her brother had found his place of peace. Despite multiple requests and threatened consequences, she remained steadfast, and the cliff of losing my temper came into view. In that moment, I managed to lower my voice and ask, "Would you find it frustrating if you were watching a little 7-year-old girl misbehave when she could be up among the flowers, playing in the fountains, and walking around the lake with her family?"

Authority and Choice

In mindfulness terms, authority in parenting is mostly about making choices moment to moment. It starts with paying attention to our breath, particularly in the challenging areas of parenting, and practicing softening our breath during the most difficult moments. This practice is about choosing how we want to respond before reaching a breaking point.

Practical Steps for Mindful Parenting

1. **Breathing Techniques**: Practice deep, mindful breathing to calm your mind and body. Focus on each inhale and exhale, allowing it to center you in the present moment.
2. **Stay Present**: Focus on being fully present during interactions with your children. Pay attention to their cues and respond with empathy and understanding.
3. **Set Clear Boundaries**: Establish clear and consistent boundaries with your children. Boundaries provide a sense of security and help children understand expectations.
4. **Reflect on Emotions**: Take time to reflect on your emotions and reactions. Understanding your triggers helps you respond more thoughtfully in challenging situations.

5. **Positive Reinforcement**: Use positive reinforcement to encourage desired behaviors. Praise your children for their efforts and accomplishments, fostering a positive and supportive environment.
6. **Practice Patience**: Cultivate patience by recognizing that both you and your children are learning and growing together. Allow yourself grace during challenging moments.
7. **Mindful Communication**: Practice mindful communication by listening actively and speaking with intention. This helps build trust and strengthens your relationship with your children.

By integrating these mindfulness practices into your parenting style, you can navigate challenges with greater ease and foster a nurturing and supportive environment for your family.

CHAPTER 27

Mindfulness and the Power of Breath

The Essence of Mindful Breathing

Mindfulness is not confined to sitting still and motionless; it is a habit that we can incorporate into our active, everyday lives. We are living, active beings, and mindfulness meditation can take many informal forms once we are in the "seat" of mindfulness. So, how can mindfulness practice help us as mothers, parents, and caregivers? Mindfulness is the formal spiritual practice of our craft. Just as elite athletes and yogis train their movements into muscle memory, we are training our minds into a state of readiness for life's challenges.

The Transformative Journey of Mindfulness

Cognitive exercises such as concentrating on the single action of breathing can help us focus our time, energy, and attention on our children and ourselves. At its most resplendent and transformative, the mindfulness journey can strip away self-imposed barriers to compassionate, loving, and dynamic caregiving. That's why simplicity and non-attachment are key in my own mindfulness journey. With my children, my practice of mindfulness is less about knowing exactly what I'm "supposed to do" and more about being present with them.

Principles of Mindfulness Practice

In an attempt to truly identify, rather than define, the essential principles of mindfulness practice, Carla Naumburg, PhD, writes: "I can't tell you what mindfulness is, but I can tell you what I practice when I sit. When I practice sitting meditation, I set the intention to keep my mind focused on one thing, such as my breath, and sit in a way that allows me to be alert and relaxed enough to nurture this intention." This simple practice, as described by Naumburg, is the spiritual path we follow. Viewing our mindfulness practice as a simple, deliberate act—one delicate breath followed by another delicate breath—reduces the odds of getting in our own way. Setting the intention to follow through with our practice increases the chances of establishing a habit.

Practical Steps for Incorporating Mindful Breathing

1. **Find a Comfortable Position**: Whether sitting, standing, or lying down, find a position that allows you to be alert and relaxed. There is no need to be motionless; mindfulness can be practiced in any position.
2. **Focus on Your Breath**: Pay attention to the sensation of your breath as it enters and leaves your body. Notice the rise and fall of your chest or the feeling of air passing through your nostrils.
3. **Set an Intention**: Set a clear intention for your practice. This could be to remain present, to cultivate patience, or simply to focus on your breath. Revisit this intention throughout your practice.
4. **Allow Thoughts to Pass**: As thoughts arise, acknowledge them without judgment and gently bring your focus back to

your breath. This practice helps train your mind to stay present.

5. **Practice Regularly**: Incorporate mindful breathing into your daily routine. Even a few minutes each day can make a significant difference in your ability to remain calm and focused.

6. **Integrate into Daily Activities**: Practice mindful breathing during everyday activities, such as walking, cooking, or playing with your children. This helps embed mindfulness into your routine and enhances your overall well-being.

By integrating these mindful breathing practices into your life, you can create a sense of calm and focus that supports you in your role as a mother, parent, and caregiver. This practice not only benefits you but also sets a positive example for your children, fostering a nurturing and mindful family environment.

CHAPTER 28

Mindfulness and the Art of Letting Be

Embracing the Practice of Letting Be

Vimala Schneider McClure beautifully describes what can happen when we settle into—and make a habit of—allowing things to be as we, and they, are. She knows, as good practitioners know, that we can't drop into such generosity indefinitely. Given the nature of strong emotions—the way they yank and pull and hurt—our capacity to be present and accepting in the face of such strong pulls and pushes is consistent only in its inconsistency. And that's all right. Acknowledging this fact is nothing short of a big step forward: an overture to shared humanity—and compassion. By admitting and accepting our foibles—not creating drama with them—we begin to see how struggle, too, can deepen our appreciation of ordinary life. By acknowledging this truism, we also reinforce a powerful mindfulness practice: letting be what's inside us, what's outside us.

The Power of Letting Be

Can we strive to be present with that awareness, even momentarily? Can we try, in McClure's words, to let "be" be? "In letting be, a mother is saying to herself, to her child, and to whatever is sticking in her that she's too busy to haul out at the moment: It's all right.

95

You're all right. So I love it all up! I'll let 'be' be." These wise lines by Vimala Schneider McClure in her book *Infant Massage* frame a practice at the heart of mindfulness. We can think of all the things we bring to mindfulness as practices: attention, compassion, joy, curiosity. All of them fall under the heading of "letting be," for it's through letting be—at its simplest, learning to be present—that we come to practice everything else.

Practical Steps for Practicing Letting Be

1. **Mindful Awareness**: Cultivate mindful awareness by being present in each moment without judgment. Allow yourself to observe thoughts and emotions without getting entangled in them.

2. **Acceptance**: Practice acceptance by acknowledging your feelings and experiences as they are. Let go of the need to control or change them, and simply let them be.

3. **Self-Compassion**: Be kind to yourself when you encounter strong emotions or challenges. Recognize that it's okay to feel what you're feeling and to have limitations.

4. **Gentle Reminders**: Use gentle reminders or mantras to bring yourself back to the present moment. Phrases like "It's all right" or "Let it be" can help ground you in acceptance.

5. **Create Space**: Give yourself the space to experience and process emotions without rushing to fix or resolve them. This space allows for natural resolution and healing.

6. **Mindful Activities**: Engage in activities that promote mindfulness, such as meditation, yoga, or nature walks. These practices help reinforce the art of letting be.

7. **Reflective Journaling**: Keep a reflective journal to explore your thoughts and feelings. Writing can be a powerful tool for understanding and accepting your inner experiences.

8. **Supportive Community**: Connect with a supportive community or mindfulness group. Sharing experiences and learning from others can reinforce your practice of letting be.

Embracing the Journey

The journey of letting be is one of continuous learning and practice. It involves embracing the present moment with compassion and openness, even when faced with strong emotions and challenges. By integrating these mindfulness practices into your daily life, you can cultivate a sense of peace and acceptance, creating a nurturing environment for yourself and your family.

CHAPTER 29

Mindfulness and the Joy of Play

Practicing Mindful Breathing

Start by sitting in a comfortable position and closing your eyes. Pay attention to your breath. Notice the coolness of the air as you inhale and the warmth as you exhale. Don't try to focus on anything else. Just breathe. Every time your thoughts wander, don't worry—it's normal. This awareness signifies how little control we often have over our attention. Imagine your thoughts as trains passing through a station. Acknowledge them, let them pass, and then gently return your focus to the stream of air flowing from your nostrils and around your nose. If your thoughts settle for a few seconds, coordinate them with your breath to signal presence.

Choosing Love Over Fear

In every moment of our lives, we have the choice between fear and love. Choosing love means deciding not to focus on worry or what we lack, but instead on gratitude, guidance, faith, and being present. Our function then becomes spreading the love and joy within us. Though it's challenging to choose love at all times, practicing mindfulness helps us stay present. By catching ourselves when we're dwelling on the past or worrying about the future and choosing to be here now, we can make this practice more natural over time.

The Joy of Children's Play

Children exemplify how we should embrace joy. They are not concerned about the future; they revel in the present moment. Observing small children at play reminds us of the pure joy that comes from being present. They see wonders we often overlook, and their open hearts make their perception liberating and inviting. Their concentration on their play is filled with joy and fun. They are fully engaged in the present moment.

Practical Steps to Foster Joy Through Mindfulness

1. **Engage in Play**: Spend time playing with your children. Engage in their activities and let yourself be fully present. This not only strengthens your bond but also helps you reconnect with the joy of play.

2. **Practice Gratitude**: Cultivate gratitude by acknowledging the small joys in your daily life. Write down things you are grateful for each day, fostering a positive mindset.

3. **Mindful Observation**: Observe your surroundings with the curiosity of a child. Notice the details, the colors, and the sounds around you. This practice helps you stay present and appreciate the moment.

4. **Let Go of Worry**: When you find yourself worrying about the future or dwelling on the past, gently bring your focus back to the present. Use mindful breathing to anchor yourself in the now.

5. **Express Love**: Make a conscious effort to express love and kindness in your interactions. Whether it's a kind word, a hug, or a smile, spreading love enhances your connection with others and fosters joy.

6. **Create Joyful Moments**: Incorporate joyful activities into your routine. This could be dancing, singing, playing games, or any activity that brings you and your children happiness.

By integrating these mindfulness practices into your daily routine, you can cultivate a sense of joy and presence, enriching your life and the lives of your children.

CHAPTER 30

Mindfulness and the Beauty of Nature

Embracing Mindful Nature Observation

To begin with mindful nature observation, stand and write down any thoughts or feelings that occur to you. Your senses will be very awakened, which is one of the key concepts of mindful nature observation. Something might surprise you or make you feel good; it's important to write these feelings down. If you also experience feelings of sadness or pain, that's okay. Observe nature mindfully. Allow yourself to be completely open to every experience that comes your way. Use all your senses and be fully present in the moment.

When you are out in nature, your concentration may improve, making it easier to be fully present. Feel how the truth of impermanence is often very clearly experienced in nature, and every little sense might feel different from the last. Shake off any remnants of expectations and see everything as it is, in all its wonder and beauty.

Practical Steps for Mindful Nature Observation

1. **Mindful Breathing**: Start by taking several slow, deep breaths. Relax and allow your mind to wander. Let thoughts

and feelings come and go without judgment. Focus on your breath and the present moment.

2. **Engage Your Senses**: Use all your senses to observe your surroundings. Notice the colors, shapes, textures, sounds, and smells. Try not to name or label anything; instead, experience it as light, dark, movement, sound, and so forth.

3. **Write Down Observations**: Stand and write down any thoughts or feelings that occur to you during your nature observation. This practice helps you become more aware of your inner experiences and how nature affects you.

4. **Find Patterns**: Notice what people are doing and try to spot patterns in their behavior. Observe the patterns in nature as well, such as the way leaves move in the wind or the flow of water in a stream.

Creating Space for Mindfulness in Nature

Find a beautiful and quiet place outdoors. Spend an entire afternoon there, if possible—especially if you live in a northern climate where such days may be limited. Leave your cell phone and other technology at home or, at the very least, turned off. If you have young children at home, you might need to do this activity in the evening and arrange for someone to care for your children. A beautiful garden or even a park can have the same effect.

Focus on Your Feelings and Thoughts: While in nature, focus mainly on your feelings and thoughts rather than on the specifics of nature itself. Allow yourself to be fully present and attuned to your inner experiences.

The Wisdom of Nature

Reflect on the Latin proverb: "If the wind will not serve, take to the oars." This reminds us that we have the power to navigate our journey, even when circumstances are not ideal. Embracing mindfulness in nature helps us cultivate resilience and a deeper appreciation for the beauty and impermanence of life.

CHAPTER 31

Mindfulness and the Power of Gratitude

The Importance of Being Present

When we mothers practice mindfulness, we are repeatedly drawn back to the present moment because that is where our children live. By being truly present with the people in our lives, we can witness much to be grateful for. The daily practice of gratitude has been shown to have a positive effect on our well-being. When shared within a community, it can help protect against stress and depression.

The Science Behind Gratitude

In the book *Mindfulness: A Practical Guide to Finding Peace in a Frantic World*, Professor Williams and Dr. Penman explain the reasoning behind this association. They argue that "Our brains are naturally wired towards noticing threat and uncertainty, but we also evolved to seek out opportunity, satisfaction, and kindness." This means that the more we actively build our awareness of life's positive aspects, the more we can buffer ourselves against stress.

The Abundant Reservoir of Compassion

In *Mindfulness for Mothers: Finding Your Own Inner Strength Helps You Nurture Your Children*, the author emphasizes the incredible capacity of the human spirit to give and love. "The reservoir for the Father and the Mother is unlimited," he says. For some, giving is at the heart of their faith, while for others, the practice of compassion is a central focus of their meditation. As parents, we often give until we think we can give no more, feeling stretched to our limits. Yet, with practice and support, we discover that the well of compassion within us is deep and refreshing.

Theresa, a friend who is a social worker in a challenging inner-city environment, shared her experience: "You give everything you can and think, 'I have nothing left. I won't be able to make it through the day.' But somehow, you do, and you still have something left for the children."

Practical Gratitude Practices

1. **Daily Gratitude Journaling**: Keep a gratitude journal and write down three things you are grateful for each day. This practice helps shift your focus to the positive aspects of your life.

2. **Gratitude Meditation**: Incorporate gratitude meditation into your mindfulness routine. Spend a few minutes each day reflecting on the things you are grateful for, allowing these feelings to fill your heart and mind.

3. **Share Gratitude with Others**: Share your gratitude with family and friends. Expressing appreciation for others strengthens relationships and creates a positive ripple effect.

4. **Mindful Observation**: Take a moment to observe and appreciate the small joys in your daily life. Whether it's the sound of birds chirping or the warmth of a hug from your child, these moments are worth acknowledging.

5. **Gratitude Rituals**: Establish gratitude rituals in your family. For example, you can make it a habit to share what each family member is grateful for during mealtime or bedtime.

By integrating these gratitude practices into your daily routine, you can enhance your well-being, foster a positive mindset, and create a nurturing environment for yourself and your family.

CHAPTER 32

Conclusion

The Path to Transformative Mindfulness

The question now is not whether we should dedicate ourselves to a daily mindfulness practice, but how to accomplish deep, transformative mindfulness that withstands the increasingly long and often challenging days. We must prepare to meet each dawn with meditation practice and grateful hearts, embracing a new, mindful energy as we go about our day. By working through the hard moments and the sublime moments with attention and intention, we simplify the stuff of life, giving ourselves time to relish and savor beauty and joy while sending love to hearts across the universe. We arrive at each parenting moment fully present, animated by a peaceful heart.

Nurturing Wholehearted Mindfulness

Together, let us nurture a powerful awareness and practice of wholehearted mindfulness in our everyday lives and in the lives of our children. While we mothers may not be able to solve all the world's problems tomorrow, by touching our inner peace every day, we accomplish a great deal. We show up in our marriages, with our families, and in our communities in positive and meaningful ways. We become courageous and lean into each moment with fierce love, uncovering the endless reservoir of peace within our hearts and pouring it into the world. This allows things to settle, clear, and bloom around us.

Attuning to Our Children's Needs

From this place of inner peace, we can attune ourselves to our children's growing needs, responding to their physical and emotional health with profound insight and love. We can show the world how to move through motherhood and life with grace, love, and peaceful fire.

www.ingramcontent.com/pod-product-compliance
Lightning Source LLC
Chambersburg PA
CBHW020535160726
47992CB00005BA/2390